For Micah Benjamin Raphael

Mazal Tov!

The Rituals and Customs of a Jewish Wedding

Rabbi Dr. Michael Shire

*Illustrated with Illuminated Manuscripts
and Ketubbot from the British Library*

Stewart, Tabori & Chang
New York

Contents

Introduction ... 9

From Ancient Times ... 12
Theology ... 14
History ... 19
Laws ... 22

The Customs of the Ceremony ... 28
A Time to be Married ... 30
Aufruf ... 31
Participants ... 32
Fasting and *Mikveh* ... 32
Bedeken and Procession ... 34
Chuppah ... 35
Circling ... 37
Marriage Blessings ... 38
Giving the Ring ... 40
Reading the *Ketubbah* ... 42
Breaking the Glass ... 45

The Wedding Service ... 46
Traditional *Ketubbah* ... 58
Alternative *Ketubbah* ... 62

Readings and Meditations ... 65
Brit (Covenant) ... 65
Ahava (Love) ... 68
Kiddushin (Holiness) ... 70

Glossary ... 74
After the Ceremony ... 76
Acknowledgments ... 77

Introduction

*G*etting married is a time of celebration as well as one of great decision and responsibility. The Jewish wedding ceremony incorporates these two aspects of marriage: on the one hand sanctity and an affirmation of love, and on the other a down-to-earth pragmatic arrangement between two people to ensure fairness, justice, and mutual responsibility. The combination of the spiritual and the practical has been a characteristic of the Jewish wedding ceremony as a meaningful rite of passage that has remained virtually unchanged for more than 2,500 years.

At heart, it is a relatively simple affair: an exchange of rings, a one-line vow under a canopy (*chuppah*) in the presence of two witnesses, and it is all over. There need be no rabbi or synagogue, no flowers, caterers or photographers. However, Jews throughout the ages have seen the wedding ceremony not just as a private affair between two individuals but as a ritual of communal importance. Marriage fulfills God's purpose that humans find companionship and fill the earth. The community gathered around the *chuppah* act as witnesses to this new potential and join in asking God to bless the union.

The Jewish wedding ceremony has changed little over the years, yet it retains a vital power and poignancy that continues to affirm love and hope in an often desperate world. The couple standing under the *chuppah* remind us all of the innocence in the Garden of Eden and the harmony, balance, and completeness of the beginning and take us forward to the future as a premonition of the Messianic Age and the harmony that will exist in days to come. For many, each *chuppah*

Page 6: The *ketubbah* of Moses and and Diamante, daughter of Ishmael from Camerano, Italy, 1680.
The marginal illustrations show Jerusalem and other biblical sites (BL MS Or. 12377R).
Right: An open Torah scroll illustrated in the Leipnik Haggadah, Altona, 1740 (BL MS Sloane 3173 f. 35v).

brings back memories of their own wedding day, often one of radiance and bliss. Past, present, and future are all wrapped up in this one ritual. There is a looking back to past generations, a focus on the needs of the particular couple standing under the *chuppah* today, and a hope for a future renewed by fresh aspirations, dreams, and generations yet to come.

As the spiritual and emotional ties are bound in a marriage contract, there is awareness that sometimes these ties are loosened. Judaism formalizes the couple's commitment to each other in legal terms and recognizes that sometimes this legal state has to be dissolved. Divorce is a painful and desperate measure, but Judaism is sufficiently grounded in reality to know that joys and sorrows are commingled in all relationships, as in life. The shattering of a glass in the ceremony reminds us of everyday life and concerns. The wedding ceremony suggests that the way in which we deal with them is part of a true relationship too.

The establishment of the *ketubbah*, the legal contract between man and wife, guaranteed rights and privileges, especially to divorced or widowed women. Long before modern "women's rights," it set a precedent and moral direction to be followed by Western civilization. Some *ketubbot* are illustrated in this book. The colorful decoration of these *ketubbot* emphasizes their meaning and significance for us. They are a legacy of the love and commitment of wedding couples from the past. All fulfill the concept of *hiddur mitzvah*— enhancing the ritual.

This book is a guide for all those who wish to participate in this enhancement. The opportunity to draw upon *minhagim* (customs) from many different cultures and ages creates a unique ceremony dedicated to each couple and their own expressions of Jewish life and understanding. I have described the history, theology, and laws concerning marriage as well as giving explanations of the many and varied wedding customs that have been incorporated into the ceremony and the preparations for it. Some of these, such as the breaking of a plate, the throwing of a glass, and wrapping the couple in a *tallith* (prayer shawl) can be dated back to the second century CE. Other rituals and liturgies arose through the centuries, often based on the local culture in which Jews lived. The richness of our history has introduced Yemenite customs of veiling the bride, Spanish customs of throwing money and sweets, Polish Hasidic customs of dancing and carrying candles, as well as American customs of quilting the *chuppah* and incorporating personal vows. To these can be added contemporary modifications such as the now familiar egalitarian nature of the ceremony with reciprocal Hebrew vows and the breaking of two glasses underfoot. All of this rich tapestry of Jewish history is available today and Jews of whatever denomination, or of none, have the opportunity to draw upon it as they choose. I have deliberately avoided labeling customs as Orthodox or Reform in order to promote the post-denominational concept of a plurality of choice for Jewish observance. At the back of this book I have included some biblical, medieval, and modern readings and texts to reflect upon and perhaps include in parts of the ceremony. They are arranged under the three prime concepts of the wedding ceremony: Covenant, Love, and Holiness.

The wedding ceremony is a ritual of transformation. You enter as one type of person, seeing the world through the eyes of a single person, and you leave the ceremony as a couple. The ceremony is the doorway into a different lifestyle, a different understanding of yourself and others, and the possible realization of your aspirations and dreams. This is the potential of the Jewish wedding ceremony; may you be inspired by it, as I was, as you embark on your journey together in life. I wish every such couple: *Mazal Tov!*

Rabbi Dr. Michael Shire

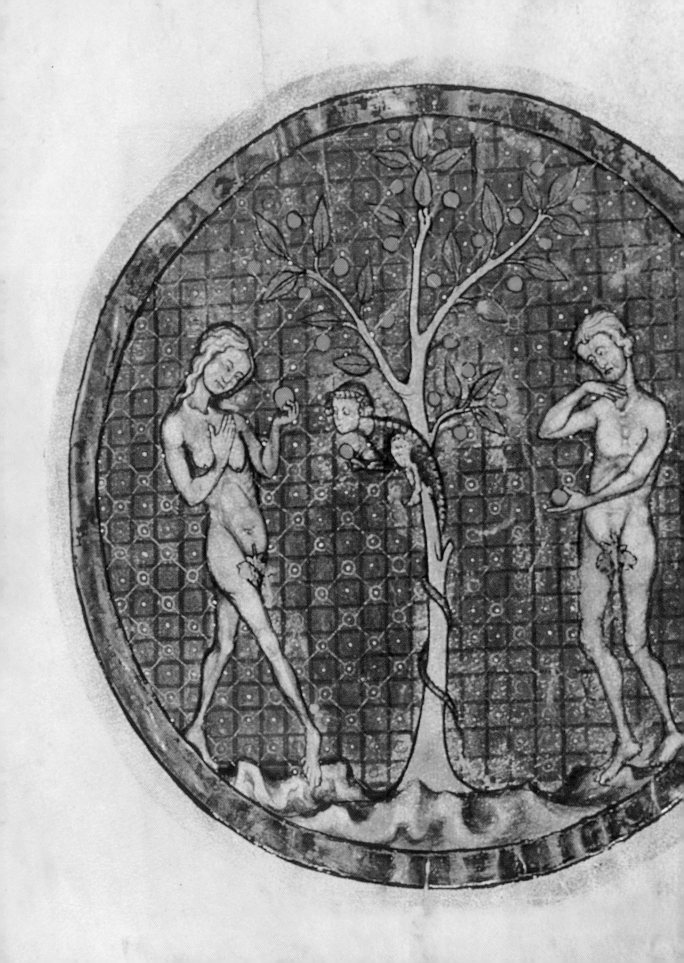

From
Ancient Times

From Ancient Times

Theology

*T*he wedding of the first couple was celebrated with pomp never repeated in the whole course of history, since God, before presenting Eve to Adam, attired and adorned her as a bride. God called to the angels saying, "Come, let us perform a service of friendship to Adam and his helpmate." The angels accordingly surrounded the marriage canopy and God pronounced the blessings upon the bridal couple. The angels then danced and played upon musical instruments before Adam and Eve in their bridal chamber.

Pirke de Rabbi Eliezer 12

From the earliest accounts of Adam and Eve in Genesis, Judaism has promoted marriage as a sacred encounter between man and woman, enshrined in a state of holiness and initiated by a sacred ceremony. To this day, Judaism seeks to bring sanctity into everyday life, and marriage is viewed as an elevation of the relationship between a man and a woman to the level of *kiddushin*—holiness.

In Judaism, the groom weds the bride in the presence of witnesses, through the exchange of a ring and a contractual document termed a *ketubbah*. In this way, husband and wife become consecrated to each other. So profound is the sanctity of marriage that it is used as a metaphor to describe the relationship between God and Israel— God as the groom and Israel as the bride. The giving of Torah on Mount Sinai, celebrated on the festival of Shavuot, is treated as a

Pages 12–13: Adam and Eve with the serpent in the Garden of Eden, an elegant Gothic miniature from the French Miscellany, northern France, about 1280 (BL MS Add. 11639 f. 520v).

betrothal ceremony wedding God to the Jewish people—with all the duties and responsibilities incumbent on both—and initiating a relationship of love and unfailing trust and faithfulness throughout the generations.

In Jewish life marriage has three purposes. Firstly, it provides for the world to be populated, in accordance with God's edict: "Be fruitful and multiply" (Genesis 1:28), which is the first commandment of the Torah. Secondly, it is an affirmation of the companionship of husband and wife and the happiness that derives from it, in accordance with Genesis 2:18: "It is not good for Man to be alone, I will make a fitting helper for him." Thirdly, it establishes new families and forms the basis of family life, as in Genesis 2:24: "Therefore a man shall leave his father and mother and cling to his wife."

In each of these ways, therefore, marriage is the fulfillment of a religious duty (*mitzvah*) and, as such, is considered to be a sacred covenant (*brit*) involving holy obligations and duties. Each partner is responsible both to the other and to God, and couples are required to build their home together as a "small sanctuary" devoted to God (Ezekiel 11:16). There is therefore a moral and religious component to marriage as well as the legal state upon which the couple agree.

In the first chapters of Genesis, the creation of the universe is interwoven with the story of the first human relationships. As the world is created, so too Adam and Eve are placed in the Garden of Eden to enjoy it. The important task of making marriages is ascribed to God, who is said to renew the work of creation continually, day by day. How does God do this? By causing marriage to take place. The rabbis of the Talmud sought to explain this through the following story:

Once, a Roman woman asked Rabbi Jose bar Halafta: "How long did it take the Holy One to create the world?" He said to her: "Six days." "What has God been doing from then until now?" "God has been occupied in making marriages." The woman said: "Even I can do that. I have men and women slaves and in an hour I can marry them off." "It may appear easy in your eyes," Rabbi Jose said, "but every marriage is as difficult for God as the dividing of the Red Sea." Then he went on his way. The woman took a thousand male slaves and a thousand female slaves and placed them in two rows, saying "This one will wed that one." In one night she married them all. The next day, they came before her—one with a wounded head, one with a bruised eye, another with a fractured arm, and one with a broken foot. "What happened to you?" she said. Each one said: "I do not want the one you gave me." Immediately the woman sent for Rabbi Jose and said to him, "Rabbi, your Torah is true, beautiful, and praiseworthy." "Indeed a suitable match may seem easy to make, yet God considers it as difficult as dividing the Red Sea," said Rabbi Jose.

Genesis Rabbah 68:4

The rabbinic literature expounds on the importance of marriage, stating: "Whoever weds a suitable woman, Elijah kisses him and God loves him" (Derekh Erets Rabbah 1). Marriage is even compared favorably to the study and practice of Torah: "He who marries a good woman is as if he fulfilled the whole Torah from beginning to end" (Yalqut Shimoni Ruth 606). Accordingly, a groom is allowed to sell a Sefer Torah in order to be able to arrange a wedding for himself. The rabbinic sages frowned upon celibacy and monasticism: "He who has no wife is not a proper man, he lives without joy, blessing, goodness, Torah, protection, and peace" (Yevamot 62b). At the birth of a child, the following blessing is recited: "May you grow up to a life of Torah, *chuppah*, and *ma'asim tovim* (good deeds)." Marriage under the *chuppah* is considered the happiest and most fulfilled state.

King David, a harp laying by his side, kneels in front of an open book. An illustration from a Haggadah copied and illuminated in Germany, 1740 (BL MS Add. 18724 f. 34v).

History

The Bible contains few descriptions of wedding ceremonies: when marriage is mentioned it is usually referred to as "taking," as in "when a man takes a wife" (Deuteronomy 24:1). However, there are several references within Genesis that indicate that some sort of festivity took place. In the story of Jacob and Leah the Bible says that "Laban gathered all the people of the place and made a feast" (Genesis 29:22). After Jacob had been tricked into marrying Leah, he had to wait until the end of the "bridal week" before he could marry Rachel (Genesis 29:27). The wedding of Isaac and Rebekah is described in more detail:

> *And Isaac went out to meditate in the field in the evening and he lifted up his eyes and saw and beheld there were camels coming. And Rebekah lifted up her eyes and when she saw Isaac, she alighted from the camel. And she said to the servant: "Who is that man that is walking in the field to meet us?" And the servant said: "It is my master." And she took her veil and covered herself. And the servant told Isaac all the things that he had done. And Isaac brought her into his mother Sarah's tent and took Rebekah and she became his wife and he loved her.*
>
> *Genesis 24:63–7*

This romantic passage sheds light on many aspects of the origins of Jewish marriage. In biblical times, fathers arranged matches for their children, although the bride's consent was asked for, as was the case when Rebekah married Isaac (Genesis 24:57–8). In the absence of a father, the responsibility fell to a brother or the steward of the house. For example, Abraham asked his steward Eliezer to search for a wife for Isaac (Genesis 24:4).

King Ahasuerus and his wife, Esther, a Gothic miniature from the exquisite French Miscellany, written and illuminated in northern France, about 1280 (BL MS Add. 11639 f. 524r).

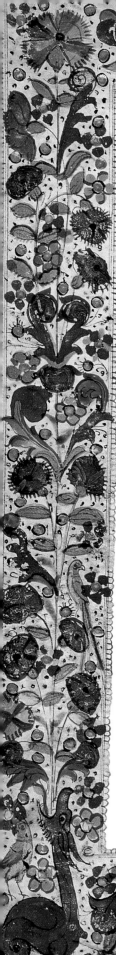

Three stages are required for Jewish marriage: engagement, betrothal, and wedding. In biblical times the terms of the engagement were made orally between fathers. The betrothal (*erusin*) necessitated the payment of a purchase price (*mohar*) by the groom or his father to the bride's father. Sometimes part of the *mohar* was given to the bride herself, together with a gift, as Shechem offers to Dinah (Genesis 34:12). Occasionally the bride brought presents from her father to the marriage as a dowry. It is thought that these transactions were recorded in a written document, though the Bible does not mention one. There is, however, one explicit mention of a document of divorce in the Bible: "Then this man rejects her, writes her a bill of divorce, hands it to her, and sends her away from his house" (Deuteronomy 24:3).

Once betrothed, the woman became the groom's legal wife, although the marriage was not consummated until the nuptial ceremony (*nissuin*), which followed a year later, or just one month later in the case of a widow. At that time, the groom, with an entourage, would escort the bride in procession from her parental home to his parental home where the *chuppah* would be erected. The wedding was accompanied by seven days of feasting and dancing.

In post-biblical times, the legal and ritual procedures for the wedding were modified and enhanced. An engagement, known as *shidduchin* or *tenaim*, was often announced with a celebration. A formal document (*sh'tar*) was created that fixed in advance the date and time of the *chuppah*, the dowry and other financial arrangements, and the compensation payable if the marriage was not taken to completion. One marriage contract, found among the Elephantine papyri in Egypt and probably dating from the fifth century BCE, carries a standard formula for the groom to recite: "I have come to your house that you may give me your daughter Mivtachiah as a wife; she is my wife and I am her husband from this day and for ever."

The Mishnah states that a wife may be acquired by any one of three ways: by money (kesef), by a document (sh'tar), or by cohabitation (bi'ah) (Mishnah Kiddushin 1:1). The second was rarely practiced and the third was ultimately forbidden, although the giving of a document and cohabitation remain aspects of the wedding. Betrothal by kesef was developed as the standard means of marriage in rabbinic law, which stated that the groom had to hand over to the bride, in the presence of two witnesses, a coin or object worth at least one perutah (a small copper coin) and to say to her the formula: "You are betrothed to me by this object." This process is known as kinyan—the physical acquisition of the bride. Since the seventh century CE, the object has come to be a ring, although in some communities in North Africa and the Near East a coin is still used. The formal vow offered today is: "Behold you are betrothed to me by this ring according to the law of Moses and Israel." Although this is recorded as far back as mishnaic times (Tosefta Ketubbot 7:6), it is not until the twelfth century that it appears as a standard part of the betrothal.

The mohar was no longer a purchase price paid to the bride's father but a charge on the husband's estate, which became payable to the wife if he divorced her or if he died. Jewish legislation concerning marriage has always striven to protect the woman prior to, within, and even subsequent to any marriage arrangement.

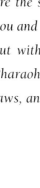

The ceremony itself underwent change too. In talmudic times the groom still escorted the bride from her father's house to his, but their entry into the *chuppah* became a symbolic act. The *chuppah* was transformed from a tent to a veil or prayer shawl spread over the heads of the bride and groom. Later, it became usual for the couple to stand under a portable canopy during the wedding ceremony. Originally, it was traditional for the Seven Blessings (see page 38) to be recited at the wedding feast. These were gradually incorporated into the service itself. In the late Middle Ages the ceremony was transferred from the home to the courtyard of the synagogue, and it became customary for the service to be conducted by a rabbi.

From the eleventh century CE, the practice began of combining *erusin* and *nissuin* in one ceremony and this became universal after the sixteenth century. There were two main reasons for this. The fate of the Jewish community being what it was at that time, it became precarious to wait a year for the consummation of the marriage. Also, it was costly to have two celebrations within a year.

Laws

*F*or you are a people consecrated to the Eternal One, your God: of all the peoples on earth the Eternal One, your God, chose you to be a distinct people. It is not because you are the most numerous of peoples that the Eternal One chose you—indeed you are the smallest of peoples; but it was because the Eternal One favored you and kept the promise God made to your ancestors whom God brought out with a mighty hand from the house of bondage, from the hand of Pharaoh, king of Egypt . . . therefore observe faithfully this Command, the laws, and the statutes that I command you this day.

Deuteronomy 7:6–8, 11

The laws governing marriage have their origin in biblical law, later expounded by the Mishnah and Talmud in the Tractate Ketubbot. The process of Jewish law has reflected changes in attitudes toward marriage over the centuries, especially in relation to women's rights. Recently, the notion of same-sex relationships has confronted Judaism and created new flexibility in Jewish law and ritual.

In biblical times preference was for marriage to relatives, emphasizing the importance of endogamy (in-marriage). Exogamy (out-marriage)

Above: An elderly man studies from an open book, most likely a volume of the *Mishnah*, from the Leipnik Haggadah, 1740 (BL MS Sloane 3173, f. 35 v.).

was seen as constituting a threat to the future of Judaism, perhaps encouraging people to leave Judaism or to fail to raise their children as Jewish. The book of Deuteronomy forbids intermarriage between the seven Canaanite Nations because they might turn people aside to worship other gods: "You shall not intermarry with them: do not give your daughters to their sons or take their daughters for your sons. For they will turn your children away from Me to worship other Gods" (Deuteronomy 7:3–4). The prophets Ezra and Nehemiah extended this prohibition to include all Gentile nations. However, the book of Ruth was in part written to demonstrate that marriage to a converted Gentile could be a noble act: here it led to the establishment of a royal lineage, the dynasty of King David. Traditionally Judaism has not approved of interfaith marriages between a Jew and a non-Jew. However, there are rabbis who will perform such marriages, citing the holiness of any committed relationship that is founded on love and on lifelong responsibility.

Biblical law allowed polygamy. For example, Jacob had two wives, as did Moses and Gideon. Solomon had seven hundred wives and three hundred concubines. As many of the stories in Genesis relate, when a man took a second wife it was often because of infertility. "Sarai, Abram's wife had borne him no children. She had an Egyptian maidservant whose name was Hagar. And Sarai said to Abram, 'Look, the Eternal One has kept me from bearing. Consort with my maid; perhaps I shall have a son through her'" (Genesis 16:1–2). Around the year 1000 CE Rabbi Gershom convened a rabbinic assembly in Germany to prohibit Jews from contracting polygamous marriages in accordance with the rabbinic dictum *dina d'malkuta dina*—the law prevailing in the land is the law for Jews too. As Christian society in

The *ketubbah* of Joseph, son of Abraham Fonari, and Malkah, daughter of Gershon, Rome, 1841. The shaped lower border features a vase with two peacocks (BL MS Or. 12377N).

בסימנא טבא ובמזלא מעליא לחתנא ולכלתא דא ׃ מצא אשה מצא מצא טוב
ויפק רצון מי"י

ברבוע

בשבת שבעה ימים לחדש כסליו שנת חמשה אלפים ושש מאות ואחת לבריאת העולם למנין שאנו מנין כֹה פֹה
רומא מתא רבתא על נהר טיב ׃ ואיך הבחור הנכבד הֹה כֹמר יוסף יצֹו החתן רֹן בן הזקן הנכבד הֹה הֹר אברהֹם
פואנרי זֹל אמר לה לנקיה ובכירה מֹרת מלכת תמא כלתא בתולתא דא בת הזקן הנכבד הֹה כֹמר נרשון חי
זֹל הוי לי לאנתו כדת מֹ וישֹ אליהון ואנכי בֹה אפלח ואוקיר ואזון ואפרנס ויתיכי כהלכת גברין יהודאין
דפלחין ומוקרין וזנין ומפרנסין ית נשיהון בקושטא וייהבנא ליכי מֹהר בתוליכי כסף זוזי מאתן רחזו ליכי
מֹד אוריתא ומזוניכי וכסותיכי וספוקיכי ומֹעל לותיכי כארחא כל ארעא וצבאת מֹרת מלכה תמא כלתא
דא והות ליה לאנתו לבֹ יוסף יצֹו החתן הֹנל ודין נדוניא דהנעלת ליה מבי נשא חמשים סקורי
לחשבון עשרה וילי הֹס ׃ מתכשיטי נשיֹ כֹבר יצֹו החתן יצֹו החתן הֹנל והוסיף לה מדיליה
וממזוניה על המהר הֹנל ישֹ עשר סקורי וחצי לחשבון הֹנל נמצא סכום כתובתא רא בין נדוניא
ותוספאה שנכ ושש ׃ סקורי והצי לחשבון הֹנל לבר מכאן זוזי רחזו לה מראוריתא וכך אֹמר
לנא כֹבר יוסף יצֹו החתן הֹנל אחריות וחומר שטר כתובתא דא קבלית עלי ועל יראתי בתֹראֹי
להתפרעא מן כל שפר ארג נכסין וקנינין ראית לי תחות כל שמיא קנינתי ודי אנא עתיד למקנא
ראית להון אחריות ואנבן דלית להון אחריות כולהון יהן אחראין וערבאין על למפרע מֹ די
סכום שטר כתובתא רא עד גמירא ואפלו מן גלימא רעל כתפאי בחיי ובמותא מן יומא דֹ ן
ולעלם וקבל עליו כֹבר יוסף יצֹו החתן הֹנל אחריות וחומר שטר כתובתא רא כאחריות וחומר כל
שטרי כתובות דנהיגי בבנות ישראל בתולות הכבודות הצנועות והכשרות דלא כאסמכתא
ורלא כטופסי דשטרי מן יומא רֹן ולעלם וקנינא מן הבחור הנכבד הֹה כֹבר יוסף יצֹו החתן
הֹנל בן הזקן הנכבד הֹה כֹבר אברהֹם פואנרי זֹל הֹנל לזכות ולתועלת הכבודה הצנועה מֹת
מלכה תמא כלתא בתולתא רא הֹנל בת הזקן הנכבד הֹה כֹבר נרשון חי זֹל הֹנל על כל מאי
דכתיב ומפורש לעילא במנא דכשר למקניא ביה והֹכל שרֹ ר וברֹ רם
ודין קיֹומיה רמלות שבעה ימים כסליו ושש מאות ואחת רֹעל הֹנד והֹכל שרֹ הֹנד והֹכל שרֹ וברֹ קיֹם

western Europe upheld monogamy, so too did Jews. However, as evidenced by the prophetic notion of comparing God's relationship with Israel to a husband's relationship to his wife, monogamy was always considered ideal. This is expounded at length in Proverbs 31. The High Priest was only allowed one wife (Leviticus 21:13–15).

A Jewish marriage must therefore be monogamous and both bride and groom must be Jewish. But there still may be impediments to marriage in Jewish law. There are classes of impediments that come under the heading *arayot* (impropriety). These consist of forbidden degrees of consanguinity (blood relationship) and affinity (relationship through marriage). These are stipulated in the Bible in Leviticus 18 and include all close relatives and those connected by marriage, except in one special case. According to the Bible (Deuteronomy 25:5–10), if a husband died leaving no children, the widow was obligated to marry her brother-in-law. This was known as a levirate marriage (*yibbum*), intended to perpetuate the deceased family name with subsequent children. The brother-in-law could exempt himself from this through the ceremony of release called *halitzah*. There are also some prohibited marriages in cases where men trace their ancestry back to priestly families (*kohanim*) of biblical times. They are traditionally prohibited from marrying widows and divorcees.

Jewish law also stipulates the conditions under which marriage is conducted. The Talmud explicitly obliges the husband to demonstrate faithfulness, respect, and love to his wife: "He who loves his wife as himself and respects her more than himself and leads his sons and daughter in the right path, of him, Scripture says, you shall know that your tent is filled with peace" (Talmud Yevamot 62b). Another rabbi states: "A man should always be careful to show respect to his wife, for blessing is found in a man's house only for the sake of his wife" (Talmud Bava Metzia 59a).

Legally, a man was required to provide his wife with food and clothing and fulfill his conjugal duties (Exodus 21:10). Conjugal rights were also held to be a religious obligation and therefore Jewish law detailed how frequently sexual relations should take place between husband and wife: every day if the husband is a man of leisure, twice a week if he is a laborer, once a week if he is an ass driver, once a month is he is a camel driver, and more than once every six months if he is a sailor (Mishnah Ketubot 5:6). However this is contingent on the prohibition of having sexual relations with a woman during her menstrual period and subsequent to it, as elaborated in the laws of family purity (*niddah*).

Divorce is regarded as a tragedy in Jewish law. Nevertheless Judaism recognizes that human relations cannot be enforced and provides a way, albeit reluctantly, for couples to dissolve their marriage. This entails the husband giving a bill of divorce (*sefer k'ritut* or *get*) to the wife in a ceremony with two witnesses. This unilateral form of divorce has become problematic in Judaism, especially if the husband refuses to grant it, leaving the wife in a position where she cannot remarry in a Jewish ceremony—this is known in Judaism as leaving her "chained" (*agunah*). Again, Jewish law continues to seek ways to retain the spirit of Jewish tradition while upholding justice in all human relationships.

The Customs
of the
Ceremony

The Customs of the Ceremony

A Time to be Married

A Jewish wedding may take place by day or by night, but there are certain days in the year on which the ceremony cannot take place. These days include Shabbat and holy days (except *Purim* and *Chanukah*, which are semi-holidays and post-biblical festivals). A wedding is not allowed to take place on Shabbat because marriage is considered a legal transaction and cannot take place on the Day of Rest. The Shabbat restriction even includes betrothals because they may lead to writing, a practice also prohibited on Shabbat.

Marriage is also forbidden on the intermediate days (*chol ha-moed*) of *Sukkot* and *Pesach*, because it is believed that one joy should not be mixed with another. The period between *Pesach* and *Shavuot*, known as the counting of the *Omer*, has traditionally also been a prohibited time due to its designation as a period of semi-mourning. This restriction also applies to the period from the fast day of the

seventeenth of Tammuz to the ninth of Av. However, today there is considerable flexibility about conducting weddings in these periods and especially on certain days within them, such as the thirty-third day of the *Omer* (*lag ba-omer*). Not all communities observe these prohibitions and some may perform marriages in these periods.

As for specific days on which one can be married, there are no set rules. However, Mishnah Ketubbot 1.1 recommends a Wednesday if the bride is a virgin and a Thursday if she is a widow or a divorcée. There is a tradition that a wedding should be held on a Tuesday, because it was on the third day of creation that the Bible repeats twice: "And God saw how good it was."

Aufruf

On the Shabbat immediately preceding the wedding day, the couple may be called up (*aliyah* in Hebrew, *aufruf* in Yiddish) to a reading of the Torah in synagogue. This is an ancient custom mentioned in rabbinic sources (Pirke de Rabbi Eliezer). In some communities rice, wheat, nuts, and candied almonds are thrown at the couple to celebrate their forthcoming marriage. The Talmud tells of how King Solomon built a gate in the Temple to honor grooms who were about to be married (Masechet Soferim 19). This is considered to be a precedent for the practice of inviting the groom to this special honor in the synagogue. Sephardi communities have an alternative custom known as *Avraham yasiv* (literally: "Abraham grew old") whereby the groom is called up to the Torah following the wedding ceremony.

Pages 28–9: Flanked by two dancing maids, Miriam the prophetess plays a timbrel decorated with a red fleur-de-lys. From a Spanish Haggadah produced about 1300 (BL MS Or. 2737, f. 86r).
Left: A *Pesach* meal, from the Barcelona Haggadah. *Pesach* is usually celebrated in the home. Marriage, by the creation of new families, sustains such sacred rituals (BL MS Add. 14761 f. 20v).

Participants

The officiant at a wedding ceremony is called a *mesadder kiddushin*. Since the Middle Ages this role has usually been performed by a rabbi although there are no legal requirements and any competent person may act as a *mesadder kiddushin*. According to rabbinic law, two witnesses are required, as well as a *minyan*—a prayer quorum of a minimum of ten people to be present during a wedding to ensure that the ceremony is public and supported by the community.

There are historical precedents for the presence of a "best man": Samson had thirty companions at his wedding (Judges 14:11), and rabbinic literature refers to *shoshvin*, the groomsmen who lead the groom to the *chuppah*. In rabbinic literature, the angels Gabriel and Michael were said to be the *shoshvin* for the marriage of Adam and Eve.

Fasting and Mikveh

There is a tradition originating in medieval Germany that the bride and groom fast from the dawn of their wedding day until the first cup of wine at the ceremony. Since the wedding day ends one phase of life and begins another it is often compared to *Yom Kippur*, a time of serious reflection and prayer marked by fasting. The wearing of a white gown (*kittel*) by the man, symbolizing a kind of innocent rebirth, accentuates this connection. In talmudic times both bride and groom wore crowns of gold or wreaths with roses, myrtles, and

A congregation of men, women, and children gather in the synagogue. From the Barcelona Haggadah, painted in the mid- to late fourteenth century (BL MS Add. 14761 f. 65 v).

olive branches. Traditionally the couple recited a confession of sins during the afternoon prayer service (*minchah*) before the wedding ceremony.

It used to be common for the bride to atend the *mikveh* (ritual immersion) prior to her wedding, in conformance with the traditional laws of family purity (*niddah*). Today both groom and bride often find special spiritual significance in each performing ritual immersion as a spiritual cleansing in preparation for a new life together. If a parent of the bride or groom is deceased, it may also be customary to visit the grave before a wedding. Alternatively, one can recite the memorial prayer (*el male rachamim*) in synagogue prior to the wedding day.

Bedeken and Procession

When the ritual of *kinyan* has been completed, the groom and his supporters dance to the bride who sits on a special chair. *Kinyan* is the signing of the *ketubbah*, accompanied by a ritual whereby the bride accepts a piece of cloth handed to her by the groom in lieu of the actual *ketubbah*, which she receives after the ceremony. The groom then performs the act of *bedeken*—covering the face of the bride with a veil. The idea of a procession is an ancient one, as bride and groom are considered king and queen for this day and should therefore be accompanied by an entourage. The veiling of the bride has its roots in the biblical story of Isaac and Rebecca. When Rebecca saw Isaac for the first time, she veiled herself (Genesis 24:65). However, it is often also connected to the story of Jacob. Laban tricked him into marrying his elder daughter, Leah, instead of his beloved Rachel (Genesis 29:16–30). The groom therefore veils the bride himself to ensure she is the correct wife!

Bedeken usually takes place in the presence of family members, immediately prior to the ceremony, just before the procession to the *chuppah*. The officiant then pronounces the blessing that was bestowed upon Rebecca before she left her home, "O Sister, May you grow into thousands of myriads" (Genesis 24:60), followed by the Blessing of all the Matriarchs: "May God make you as Sarah, Rebecca, Rachel, and Leah."

Chuppah

*I*n ancient times, the groom would escort the bride in joyful procession from her parental home to his parental home, where the wedding feast would be held. There, in a special chamber known as the *chuppah*, built by the groom's father, the marriage would be consummated, as recorded in the Bible: "It is like a groom emerging out of the *chuppah* rejoicing as a hero in order to run a race" (Psalms 19:5).

In talmudic and medieval times, the *chuppah* became a symbol of intimacy and protection. At first, the specially constructed *chuppah* was replaced by a *tallith* (prayer shawl), spread over the heads of the bride and groom in accordance with the words of Ruth to Boaz: "Spread thy cloak over thy handmaid" (Ruth 3:9). It later became the practice for the couple to stand under a portable canopy during the wedding ceremony. In the fourteenth century, the ceremony was transferred from the home to the synagogue courtyard or the synagogue itself and it became customary for the service to be conducted by a rabbi. The popularity of the outdoor *chuppah* in the grounds of the synagogue was justified by a sixteenth-century codifier of Jewish law, Rabbi Moshe Isserles, who commented: "Some say that the *chuppah* should be set up under the sky as a good omen that their children will be as numerous as the stars" (Shulchan Aruch, Even Ha-Ezer 61:1). In some parts of Germany, one of the outside walls of the synagogue includes a "*chuppah* stone," at which the wedding cup was thrown after the ceremony instead of being smashed underfoot.

The *chuppah* today consists of a roof of silk or satin supported by four poles under which the bridal couple and their immediate family stand during the wedding ceremony. As the bride and groom are considered to be royal on this special day, purple cloth—symbolic of royalty—is often used. There is a rabbinic tradition of planting a pine tree to mark the birth of a daughter and a cedar for the birth of a son. For the marriage ceremony, branches would be cut from the couple's trees and carved to make the poles of the *chuppah* (Talmud Gittin 57a). The poles may be fixed to the ground or held by four people specially chosen for this role named *unterferers*—supporters.

The *chuppah* today may be interpreted as a symbol of the home that the bride and groom are about to establish and as an expression of the hope that it will be filled with God's presence. The fact that the *chuppah* is open on all sides recalls the tent of Abraham, who is considered the exemplar of hospitality in the Bible (Genesis 18). His

tent was open on all sides so that he could invite passing strangers to eat. The *chuppah* may be decorated or inscribed with appropriate sayings, the most popular being the traditional verse from the Talmud: "The voice of joy and the voice of gladness, the voice of the bride and the voice of the groom" (Ketubbot 8a). The *chuppah* is a symbol of the Jewish wedding and, if it is made specially, can then adorn the couple's home as a symbol of the establishment of a sacred and loving space. Some are framed and hung on a wall, other larger *chuppahs* may be quilted and hung over the marriage bed.

Circling

The groom is led to the *chuppah* by his father and the bride's father. He then stands under the *chuppah* and waits for the bride to join him on his right, in accordance with Psalm 45:10: "The queen stands at your right hand." The bride is customarily accompanied by her mother and the groom's mother, although the tradition of the father accompanying the bride is also often practiced. An alternative custom is for the women to carry lighted candles to the *chuppah*. The practice of the groom entering first and waiting for his bride is said to be a reference to the enactment of the Covenant with the Israelites at Mount Sinai, when God "came from Sinai to receive Israel as a groom goes out to meet a bride" (Mekhilta Bachodesh 3).

Traditionally the bride is led round the groom three or seven times, according to preference, as she enters under the *chuppah*. This evokes the biblical verse: "A woman shall go round a man" (Jeremiah 31:22).

Right: The *chuppah* is raised up high by the *unterferers*, from Liturgical Selections, a manuscript containing prayers and blessings for special occasions, England, 1714 (BL MS Harley 5713, f. 17v). Pages 38–9: Also from Liturgical Selections, a singing lesson, with musicians in fashionable eighteenth-century synagogue dress (BL MS Harley 5713 f. 4v).

Three is the number of times that the phrase "I will betroth you" is proclaimed in Hosea 2:21–23, while seven is the number of biblical verses that contain the phrase "and when a man takes a wife." This ritual may have originally symbolized the exclusivity of the groom to the bride. Nowadays, however, this action may be shared by both bride and groom, taking turns to circle each other. One kabbalistic interpretation suggests that the souls of the bride and groom gradually become intertwined in their circling. The couple are then welcomed under the *chuppah* with the words of Psalm 118: "Blessed be those who come in the name of the Eternal One. We bless you from the house of God."

Marriage Blessings

Each part of the marriage ceremony—*erusin* and *nissuin*—has its own special wedding blessing to be recited. The betrothal blessing is recited immediately before the giving of the ring: it is recorded in the Talmud (Ketubbot 7b) and thanks God for the

sanctification of marriage under the *chuppah*. It is normally recited over a cup of wine to symbolize the joy of the occasion of the betrothal. It has become customary for the bride's mother to offer the cup to the bride and groom. This cup of wine is sometimes shared by all standing under the *chuppah* as a symbol of the joy shared by the family and the couple. The second blessing is known as *birkat chatanim*—literally, the groom's blessing—and is recited after the reading of the *ketubbah*. Also recorded in the Talmud (Ketubbot 8a), it consists of six individual blessings. Together with the repeated blessing over the wine, these are termed the *sheva brachot*—the seven blessings. The second cup of wine is reserved only for the bride and groom as their relationship is reserved only for each other.

The *sheva brachot* may be recited by seven guests or sung by a soloist. There is a custom of Sephardic origin that the bride and groom be draped in a *tallith* as the blessings are recited. The blessings contain a reference to the first human encounter in the Garden of Eden, when life was complete and perfect. They also express hope for the end of days, when life will

become perfect yet again. In the meantime, a glimpse of that perfect world is revealed at each wedding ceremony as two people reenact that first encounter in perfect time. The *sheva brachot* refer to them as "groom together with bride" and "groom and bride," thus indicating the importance of their continued individuality even as they come together in marriage.

Giving the Ring

The central act of the wedding ceremony is the giving of a ring accompanied by a declaration of betrothal. It is generally accepted, though not universally required, that

the ring should be made of precious metal, unadorned with stones, and unpierced. This is to avoid any misrepresentation of its value and to symbolize the wholeness of the couple in marriage and the hope for an unbroken union. The kabbalists viewed the ring as a symbol of a circle of light that revealed the mystery of men and women coming together in marriage.

Traditionally the ring should belong to the groom, but he may borrow one if the bride is aware that he has done so. It is placed on the bride's index finger, where tradition claims a direct link via an artery between the finger and the heart. Later it is transferred to the third finger, on which it will be permanently worn.

The giving of the ring is accompanied by a declaration of betrothal in both Hebrew and English, which states: "Behold, you are betrothed to me by this ring according to the law of Moses and Israel." The bride traditionally had a passive role in the acceptance of the ring with a verse from the Song of Songs, but nowadays she may also offer a ring in exchange, thus demonstrating the egalitarian nature of the wedding and of the relationship with a declaration of betrothal. These declarations may also be accompanied by personal vows of commitment, love, or devotion.

In parts of medieval Europe it was customary for the groom to place a large silver ring, intricately designed in the shape of a house or the Jerusalem Temple, on his bride's finger. The ring symbolized the home that the bride and groom would make in their future lives together. This ring was then replaced by a simple ring of precious metal as the permanent marriage token.

From Liturgical Selections: The bridegroom prepares to place the ring on the bride's finger, while reciting the betrothal formula. The ring is large, but unadorned (BL MS Harley 5713 f. 17 v).

Reading the Ketubbah

The Jewish marriage contract has its origins in the second century CE, during the time of the compilation of the Mishnah and Talmud. According to biblical law, a husband is allowed to divorce a wife at his own discretion without any further obligation (Deuteronomy 24:1). The rabbis, concerned over the ease of divorce, decided to provide protection for the wife's social and financial interest if a divorce decree was issued. They thus instituted a mandatory marriage contract known as a *ketubbah*. The first *ketubbot* were written in Aramaic, the common language of second-century Judaism. The earliest surviving *ketubbah* was found in documents retrieved from the Dead Sea Scrolls caves. It belonged to a woman named Babata who considered it so significant and important in her life that she took it with her as a treasured possession when she hid from persecution in the Judean hills.

It was not until the Middle Ages that the standard wording emerged. This stipulated the groom's obligations to safeguard his wife's rights, including protecting her against arbitrary divorce and guaranteeing provision for her should the marriage be dissolved or she be made a widow. These financial sums, as well as the sums brought to the marriage by the bride as a dowry, were all stipulated in the *ketubbah*. The *ketubbah* also states other requirements of the groom such as the provision of food, clothing, and conjugal rights. The *ketubbah* calls for a formal transaction as proof of the acceptance of the marriage proposal (*kabbalat kinyan*). This took the form of a strip of cloth that was held by the bride and groom, connecting them together as the *ketubbah* is jointly signed. Signing the *ketubbah* can take place prior

The *ketubbah* of Moses ben Judah from Ascoli and Ester, daughter of Joshua Sabbetai. Ancona, Italy, 1776. The borders are illustrated with the signs of the zodiac (BL MS Or. 12377M).

אשתך תהיה... ישרת בעלה

בריבועי בשבת ארבעה עשר יום לחדש ניסן שנת חמשת אלפים וחמש מאות ושלשים ושש לבריאת עולם למנין שאנו מנין כאן אנקונא מתא דיתבא על כיף ימא ועל נהרי
אסף ופומושינו הבחור המפואר כ"הר משה מיכאל יצ"ו בן הישר הנעלה המשכיל וגבון כ"הר יהודא
החבר כמוהר יהושע שבתי מאסקולי יצ"ו הין לי לאנתו כרת משה וישראל ואנא בסייעתא דשמיא
אפלח ואוקיר ואזון ואפרנס ואכסה יתיכי כהלכת גוברין יהודאין דפלחין ומוקרין וזנין ומפרנסין ומכסין
לנשיהון בקושטא ויהיבנא ליכי מהר בתוליכי כסף זוזי מאתן דחזי ליכי מדאורייתא ומזוניכי וספוקיכי
ומיעל לותיכי כאורח כל ארעא ובאת מרת אסתר בת כלתא בתולתא דא יהות לה לכר משה
מיכאל חתן דנן יצ"ו הנ"ל לאנתו ודן נדוניא דהנעלת ליה מבי אבוה שש מאות סקורי לעדר עשרה
פאולי הסקורי וההנומאותם סקורי מכל בלבמעות מחושבים ומאה סקורי כל בכך עדיי ויהב וכסף ומרגליות
טובות ושלש מאות סקורי כנגד בכל צמר ופשתן ומשי וכסי שיני נשים ושמושי ערש וצבי כהר
משה מיכאל חתן דנן יצ"ו הנ"ל והוסיף לה מן דיליה ליה ממוניה על המותר הנ"ל מאה ועשרים סקורי כל
נמצא סכום כתובתא דא בין נדוניא ותוספתא שבע מאות ועשרים סקורי כנגד לכל ממאתן זוזי דחזי לה
דאינון עקר הכתובה דכך אמר לא כהר משה מיכאל חתן דנן יצ"ו הנ"ל אחרית כתובתא דא ותוספת רא
קבילית עלי ועל ירתאי בתראי להתפרעא מן כל שפר ארג נכסין וקנינין דאית לי תחות כל שמיא די
קנינא ורעתיד אנא למקנא נכסין ראית להון אחריות ודלית להון אחריות כלהון יהון אחראן וערבאן על
לפרוע כתובתא דא ותוספת דא עד מרא ואפילו מן גלימא דעל כתפאי בחיי ולאחר חיי מן יומא
דנן ולעלם וקבל עליו כהר משה מיכאל חתן דנן יצ"ו הנ"ל חומר שטר כתובתא דא ותוספתא זו כחומר
כל שטרי כתובות דנהיגין בבנת ישראל העשויות כתקנת הצנועות והשרות העשוויין כתקנין חז"ל
דלא כאסמכתא ודלא כטופסי דשטרי וקנינא אנן סהדי דיי חתמן לתחא מן כהר משה מיכאל
חתן דנן יצ"ו הנ"ל בן היקר הנעלה המשכיל וגבון כהר יהודא מאסקולי יצ"ו לבנועה מרת אסתר
בת כלתא בתולתא דא אנתתיה הנ"ל בת היקר הנעלה מעלת החבר כמוהר יהושע שבתי
מאסקולי יצ"ו הנ"ל על כל מאי דכתיב ומפרש לעילא במנא דכשר

שמשון כהן פאס טורתורוש ס"ט
יעקב מ... פבלקפורן ס"ט

[lower cursive text paragraph]

שמשון כהן פאס טורתורוש ס"ט
יעקב מ... פבלקפורן ס"ט

אם אשכחך ירושלם תשכח ימיני

בסימנא טבא ובמזלא יאי"א ובנחשא מעלייא ובשעת רצון והצלחה

לנו ולכל ישראל אמן, מצא אשה מצא טוב ויפק רצון מיי ובית והון

נחלת אבות ומי" אשה משכלת נ" ;

ברביעי בשבת ארבעה עשר יום לחדש תשרי שנת חמשת אלפים ושש מאות וששה ושבעים ושבע מאות ושכ...
...שבעים לחרבן בית המקדש שיבנה במהרה בימינו ובזמ' זה כל ישראל אנחנו מנין לכמות בו מן עיר קורפו יש... דיתבא
על כיף ימא ומימיכי מעינותיכא מסתפקא מצרים אתון וחתומי מטה כזה שהיה בפנינו איך הכבד ונעלה כ"ה ר' זכריה משטאקי יל... בן
הנכבד ונעלה כהר יעקב מושטאקי יל אמר לה לבחורתא בתולתא יקירתא שפירתא צפורה בת הנכבד ונעל...
כהר חיים אקי יל הוי לי לאנתו כדת משה וישראל ואנא במימרא ... ... אפלח ואוקיר ואיזון ואסובר ...
...
לטר זכריה מושטאקי יל חתנא דנא לאנתו וקבילת עלה לבבדו ... בתוהרה ובכשמוש ... כל בנת ישראל ... ...
...
וקנינא מידי הנכבד ונעלה כהר זכריה מושטאקי יל חתנא דנא קני גמור ושלם ... דכשר למקני ביה לקיים ולאשר
על כל מאי דכתיב ומפורש לעיל ... והכל שריר ... וקיים

...בר ר' אלחנן די מ... חיים

to the wedding ceremony or immediately after it. In modern times, the wording has been adapted to reflect the egalitarian nature of modern marriage, often containing personalized language for each couple.

Breaking the Glass

The Talmud (Berachot 30b) relates that a fourth-century Babylonian rabbi, Mar bar Rabina, became so outraged at the behavior of the guests at his son's wedding that he took a precious glass and smashed it. Talmudic commentators in the twelfth and thirteenth centuries (Tosafot) suggested that this is why it became customary to break a glass at weddings. However, this is probably an interpretation of a custom already long shrouded in obscurity. It could have been a superstitious act to frighten off evil spirits. Another interpretation, found in a liturgical compendium of the fourteenth century (Kol Bo), is the notion that the glass is broken in order to recall the destruction of Jerusalem. For many couples today, it is regarded as a reminder, at a time of great joy, that there is also suffering in the world even for a loving couple. Just as the smashing of the glass is irrevocable and permanent, so too will the marriage last for ever. An alternative custom, common in eastern Europe, was for the bride and groom to attempt to stand on each other's foot, each seeking dominance over the other.

The breaking of the glass is followed by a resounding "Mazal tov!" from the entire congregation. This is followed by the final benediction.

Left: The *ketubbah* of Zechariah, son of Jacob Mustaki and Zippora, daughter of Haim Akki, Corfu, 1846 has colorful decorations and a scalloped upper border enhanced with a six-petal rosette (BL MS Or. 12377B).
Pages 46–7: The imposing *ketubbah* of Ephraim Sanguini and Luna Faro, written at Modena, Italy, on 1 October 1557 and decorated with zodiacal signs (BL MS Or. 6706).

קול ששון וקול שמחה
קול חתן וקול כלה

בסימנא טבא ובמזלא מעליא

בששי בשבת שבעה ימים לחדש חשון שנת חמשת אלפים ושלש מאות ושמנה עשרה
לבריאת העולם למנין שאנחנו מנין בו פה מודונא מתא דיתבא על נהר קיק ופאנ״ארו
ומי מעינות בא הבחור כמהר אפרים יצ״ו בכמהר קולונימוס סנגויני יצ״ו ואמר לה לבחורה
הכבודה וצנועה פרת לונא תמא בת מעלת הרופא כמהר מרדכי פאנו יצ״ו הוי לי לאינתו
כדת משה וישראל ואנא בס״ד אפלח ואוקיר ואיזון ואפרנס ואכסה יתיכי כהלכת גוברין
יהודאין דפלחין ומוקרין וזנין ומפרנסין ומכסין ית נשיהון בקושטא ויהבנא ליכי מהר
בתוליכי כסף זוזי מאתן דחזו ליכי ומזוניכי וכסותיכי וסיפוקיכי ומיעל לותיכי כאורח כל
ארעא ורביאת הבתורה מרת לונא בתולתא דא הות לה לאנתו לכמהר אפרים יצ״ו חתן
דנן וזן נדוניא דהנעלת ליה מבי אבוה עשרין לשרין של כסף צרוף וצבי כמהר אפרים יצ״ו
חתן דן ואוסיף לה ממומניה עשרין לשרין של כסף צרוף נמצא סכום כתובתא דאכין
נדוניא ותוספא ארבעין לטרין של כסף צרוף בר מכאני זוזי דחזו לה וכך אמר לנא כמהר
אפרים יצ״ו חתן דנן דנא אחריות וחומר כתובתא דא נדוניא ותוספא קבליית עלי ועל ירתאי בתראי
להתפרעא מן כל שפר ארג נכסין וקנינין דאית לי תחות כל שמיא ודעתיד אנא
למקני נכסין דאית להון אחריות ואגבן דלית להון אחריות דכולהון יהון אחראין וער״בא
מיפרע מנהון שטר כתובתא דא נדוניא ותוספא ואפילו מן גלימא דעל כתפאי בחיי ובמותא
מן יומא דן ולעלם ואחריות וחומר כתובתא דא נדוניא ותוספא קבל עליו כמהר אפרים יצ״ו
חתן דנן כאחריות וחומר כל שטרי כתובות דנהיגי בבנות ישראל הבתולות הצנועות הכשרות
העשויין כתקון חז״ל דלא כאסמכתא ודלא כטופסי דשטרי וקנינא אנן סהדי דחדרמ״י
לתתא מן כמהר אפרים יצ״ו חתן דנן לזכות הבחורה הרת לונא דא מבת על כל מאי
דכתיב ומפרש לעיל במנא דכשר למקניא ביה והכל שריר וקיים

נאם יהושע בכה״ר יהודה חלצ״ו כהן פה מודונא נאום

נאום ...

The Wedding Service

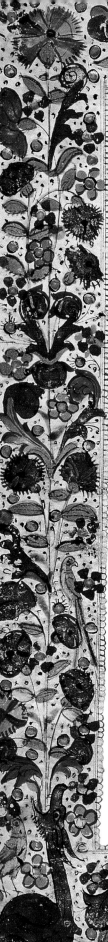

The Wedding Service

(Sections in *italics* are optional.)

The groom stands under the *chuppah*.
The bride enters and all rise.

Psalm 100

Shout for joy, all the earth,
Serve the Eternal One with gladness:
Come into God's presence with singing.
Know that the Eternal One is God,
the One who made us, to whom we belong,
whose people and whose flock we are.
Enter God's gates with thanksgiving,
God's courts with praise.
Praise God, bless God's name,
For the Eternal One is good,
God's love is everlasting,
And God's faithfulness is for all generations.

The bride and groom are welcomed at the *chuppah*.

Psalm 118:26–9

Blessed are those who come in the name of the Eternal One:
We bless you from the house of the Eternal One.

סֵדֶר קִדּוּשִׁין וְנִשּׂוּאִין

הָרִיעוּ לַיהֹוָה כָּל־הָאָרֶץ;
עִבְדוּ אֶת־יְהֹוָה בְּשִׂמְחָה;
בֹּאוּ לְפָנָיו בִּרְנָנָה.
דְּעוּ כִּי־יְהֹוָה הוּא אֱלֹהִים,
הוּא־עָשָׂנוּ וְלוֹ אֲנַחְנוּ,
עַמּוֹ וְצֹאן מַרְעִיתוֹ.
בֹּאוּ שְׁעָרָיו בְּתוֹדָה,
חֲצֵרֹתָיו בִּתְהִלָּה.
הוֹדוּ־לוֹ, בָּרְכוּ שְׁמוֹ.
כִּי־טוֹב יְהֹוָה, לְעוֹלָם חַסְדּוֹ,
וְעַד־דֹּר וָדֹר אֱמוּנָתוֹ.

בָּרוּךְ הַבָּא בְּשֵׁם יְהֹוָה.   בֵּרַכְנוּכֶם מִבֵּית יְהֹוָה:

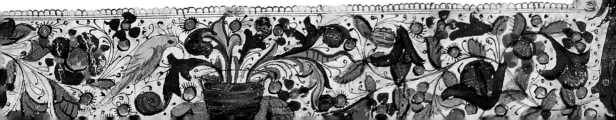

The Eternal One is God.
You have given us light.
Order the festival procession with boughs even unto
    the horns of the altar.
You are my God and I will praise you,
You are my God and I will exalt you.
Praise the Eternal One, for God is good,
God's steadfast love is eternal.

The ritual of circling.

Hosea 2:21–3

I will betroth you to me forever,
I will betroth you to me in righteousness,
And justice, love, and compassion,
I will betroth you to me in faithfulness,
And so you will know God.

Sixteenth-century wedding hymn

May the One who is supreme above all,
Who is blessed above all,
Who is great above all,
May God bless the groom and the bride.

Erusin
The Blessings of Betrothal (the first cup of wine)

Blessed are You, Source of all life, creating the fruit of the vine

Blessed are You, Source of all life, making us holy through Your

אֵל יְהֹוָה וַיָּאֶר לָנוּ אִסְרוּ־חַג בַּעֲבֹתִים עַד קַרְנוֹת הַמִּזְבֵּחַ:
אֵלִי אַתָּה וְאוֹדֶךָּ אֱלֹהַי אֲרוֹמְמֶךָּ: הוֹדוּ לַיהֹוָה כִּי־טוֹב כִּי
לְעוֹלָם חַסְדּוֹ:

וְאֵרַשְׂתִּיךְ לִי לְעוֹלָם וְאֵרַשְׂתִּיךְ לִי בְּצֶדֶק וּבְמִשְׁפָּט וּבְחֶסֶד

וּבְרַחֲמִים: וְאֵרַשְׂתִּיךְ לִי בֶּאֱמוּנָה וְיָדַעַתְּ אֶת־יְהֹוָה:

מִי אַדִּיר עַל הַכֹּל, מִי בָּרוּךְ
עַל הַכֹּל, מִי גָּדוֹל עַל הַכֹּל,
הוּא יְבָרֵךְ הֶחָתָן וְהַכַּלָּה.

בִּרְכַּת אֵרוּסִין

בָּרוּךְ אַתָּה יְיָ, אֱלֹהֵינוּ מֶלֶךְ
הָעוֹלָם, בּוֹרֵא פְּרִי הַגָּפֶן.
בָּרוּךְ אַתָּה יְיָ, אֱלֹהֵינוּ מֶלֶךְ
הָעוֹלָם, אֲשֶׁר קִדְּשָׁנוּ בְּמִצְוֹתָיו
וּמְקַדֵּשׁ עַמּוֹ יִשְׂרָאֵל עַל־יְדֵי
חֻפָּה וְקִדּוּשִׁין.

Commandments and making Your people Israel holy by the ceremony of the chuppah and the sanctity of marriage.

Blessed are You, Source of all life,
making us holy through Your Commandments and commanding us
concerning prohibited and permissible marriages, guiding us in our
relationships toward commitment and marriage under a chuppah.
Blessed are You, making Your people Israel holy by the ceremony of the
chuppah and the sanctity of marriage.

The bride and the groom exchange personal vows.

The Exchange of Rings

The groom says to the bride, as he places the ring on the forefinger of the bride's right hand:

By this ring, you are consecrated to me according to the law of Moses and Israel.

The bride says to the groom, as she places the ring on the forefinger of the groom's right hand:

By this ring, you are consecrated to me according to the law of Moses and Israel.

The bride says to the groom:

I am my beloved's and my beloved is mine. (Song of Songs 2:16)

Address to the bride and groom.

The reading of the *ketubbah*.

בָּרוּךְ אַתָּה יְיָ, אֱלֹהֵינוּ מֶלֶךְ הָעוֹלָם,
אֲשֶׁר קִדְּשָׁנוּ בְּמִצְוֹתָיו וְצִוָּנוּ
עַל הָעֲרָיוֹת, וְאָסַר לָנוּ אֶת הָאֲרוּסוֹת,
וְהִתִּיר לָנוּ אֶת הַנְּשׂוּאוֹת לָנוּ עַל יְדֵי חֻפָּה וְקִדּוּשִׁין.
בָּרוּךְ אַתָּה יְיָ, מְקַדֵּשׁ עַמּוֹ יִשְׂרָאֵל עַל יְדֵי
חֻפָּה וְקִדּוּשִׁין.

הֲרֵי אַתְּ מְקֻדֶּשֶׁת לִי בְּטַבַּעַת זוֹ כְּדַת מֹשֶׁה וְיִשְׂרָאֵל.

הֲרֵי אַתָּה מְקֻדָּשׁ לִי בְּטַבַּעַת זוֹ כְּדַת מֹשֶׁה וְיִשְׂרָאֵל.

דּוֹדִי לִי וַאֲנִי לוֹ.

Nissuin
The Sheva Brachot (the second cup of wine)

Blessed are You, Source of all life,
for creating the fruit of the vine.

Blessed are You, Source of all life,
every aspect of Your creation honors You.

Blessed are You, Source of all life,
for calling humanity into being.

Blessed are You, Source of all life,
fashioning us in Your image, after Your example, and giving us
through marriage the opportunity for commitment in life together.
We praise You Adonai, our God, for creating us.

Zion, once faced with hopelessness, shall now rejoice as her
children gather with joy in her midst. Blessed are You, Source of all
life, causing Zion to rejoice in her children.

May these two, lovers and friends, find bliss as did the first human
couple in the Garden of Eden. May these, Your children, build a
worthy home to honor Your name. Blessed are You, Source of all
life, for the happiness of the groom and bride.

Blessed are You, Source of all life,
for creating exultation and joy, groom and bride, merriment and
song, delight and rejoicing, love and closeness, peace and friendship.
Soon, may the streets of Jerusalem, as everywhere, reverberate with

ברכות נשואין:

שבע ברכות

בָּרוּךְ אַתָּה יְיָ, אֱלֹהֵינוּ מֶלֶךְ הָעוֹלָם
בּוֹרֵא פְּרִי הַגָּפֶן.

בָּרוּךְ אַתָּה יְיָ, אֱלֹהֵינוּ מֶלֶךְ הָעוֹלָם
שֶׁהַכֹּל בָּרָא לִכְבוֹדוֹ.

בָּרוּךְ אַתָּה יְיָ, אֱלֹהֵינוּ מֶלֶךְ הָעוֹלָם
יוֹצֵר הָאָדָם.

בָּרוּךְ אַתָּה יְיָ, אֱלֹהֵינוּ מֶלֶךְ הָעוֹלָם
אֲשֶׁר יָצַר אֶת הָאָדָם בְּצַלְמוֹ. בְּצֶלֶם דְּמוּת תַּבְנִיתוֹ.
וְהִתְקִין לוֹ מִמֶּנּוּ בִּנְיַן עֲדֵי עַד.
בָּרוּךְ אַתָּה יְיָ, יוֹצֵר הָאָדָם.

שׂוֹשׂ תָּשִׂישׂ וְתָגֵל הָעֲקָרָה בְּקִבּוּץ בָּנֶיהָ
לְתוֹכָהּ בְּשִׂמְחָה. בָּרוּךְ אַתָּה יְיָ,
מְשַׂמֵּחַ צִיּוֹן בְּבָנֶיהָ.

שַׂמֵּחַ תְּשַׂמַּח רֵעִים הָאֲהוּבִים, כְּשַׂמֵּחֲךָ
יְצִירְךָ בְּגַן עֵדֶן מִקֶּדֶם.
בָּרוּךְ אַתָּה יְיָ, מְשַׂמֵּחַ חָתָן וְכַלָּה.

בָּרוּךְ אַתָּה יְיָ אֱלֹהֵינוּ מֶלֶךְ הָעוֹלָם,
אֲשֶׁר בָּרָא שָׂשׂוֹן וְשִׂמְחָה, חָתָן וְכַלָּה, גִּילָה
רִנָּה דִּיצָה וְחֶדְוָה, אַהֲבָה וְאַחֲוָה וְשָׁלוֹם וְרֵעוּת.
מְהֵרָה יְיָ אֱלֹהֵינוּ יִשָּׁמַע בְּעָרֵי

joyous sounds, with merriment and joy, with groom and bride, of happy couples emerging from the chuppah with their friends in celebration. Blessed are You, Source of all life, for the happiness that the groom and bride find in each other.

Final Benediction

Our God and God of our ancestors, may this couple be blessed with the threefold blessing of the Torah:
May God bless you and keep you
May God look kindly upon you and be gracious to you
May God reach out to you in tenderness and give you a life of peace.

The breaking of the glass.

Mazal Tov!

The married couple depart the *chuppah* for the ritual of *yihud*.

Psalm 150

Praise God!
Praise God in God's holy place
Praise the one whose power the heavens proclaim,
Whose might and greatness shall be extolled.
Praise God with the shofar blast
Praise God with harp and lyre
Praise God with timbrel and dancing
Praise God with strings and pipe.
Praise God with cymbals sounding
Praise God with cymbals resounding
Let every soul praise the Eternal One.
Praise God!

יְהוּדָה וּבְחֻצוֹת יְרוּשָׁלַיִם קוֹל שָׂשׂוֹן וְקוֹל
שִׂמְחָה, קוֹל חָתָן וְקוֹל כַּלָּה, קוֹל מִצְהֲלוֹת
חֲתָנִים מֵחֻפָּתָם וּנְעָרִים מִמִּשְׁתֵּה נְגִינָתָם.
בָּרוּךְ אַתָּה יְיָ, מְשַׂמֵּחַ חָתָן עִם הַכַּלָּה.

אֱלֹהֵינוּ וֵאלֹהֵי אֲבוֹתֵינוּ וְאִמּוֹתֵינוּ, בָּרְכֵנוּ
בַּבְּרָכָה הַמְשֻׁלֶּשֶׁת הַכְּתוּבָה בַּתּוֹרָה:
יְבָרֶכְךָ יהוה וְיִשְׁמְרֶךָ.
יָאֵר יְהֹוָה פָּנָיו אֵלֶיךָ וִיחֻנֶּךָּ.
יִשָּׂא יְהֹוָה פָּנָיו אֵלֶיךָ וְיָשֵׂם לְךָ שָׁלוֹם.

הַלְלוּיָהּ!
הַלְלוּ־אֵל בְּקָדְשׁוֹ.
הַלְלוּהוּ בִּרְקִיעַ עֻזּוֹ,
הַלְלוּהוּ בִגְבוּרֹתָיו,
הַלְלוּהוּ כְּרֹב גֻּדְלוֹ.
הַלְלוּהוּ בְּתֵקַע שׁוֹפָר.
הַלְלוּהוּ בְּנֵבֶל וְכִנּוֹר.
הַלְלוּהוּ בְּתֹף וּמָחוֹל.
הַלְלוּהוּ בְּמִנִּים וְעוּגָב.
הַלְלוּהוּ בְצִלְצְלֵי־שָׁמַע,
הַלְלוּהוּ בְּצִלְצְלֵי תְרוּעָה.
כֹּל הַנְּשָׁמָה תְּהַלֵּל יָהּ.
הַלְלוּיָהּ!

Traditional Ketubbah

On the _____ day of the week, on the _____ day of the month _____, in the year _____ since the creation of the world, according to the era by which we reckon here in the town of _____ _____ known as _____, son of _____ known as _____, said to the virgin _____, daughter of _____, known as _____: "Be my wife according to the law of Moses and Israel, and I will work for you, and I will honor, support, and maintain you after the manner of Jewish husbands, who work for their wives, honor, support, and maintain them in truth.

And I will give you the bridal price [*mohar*] of two hundred *zuzim* in respect for your virginity as laid down in the Torah, as well as your food, clothing, and necessaries; and I will live with you according to universal custom."

And _____, the said virgin, consented and became his wife.

And the dowry [*nedunya*] that she inherited from her father's house—in silver, gold, valuables, clothes, and bedding—amounted to _____.

And the bridegroom, _____, added thereto an equivalent amount.

And the bridegroom, _____, declared: "I will take upon myself and my heirs after me the responsibility for this basic amount [*ketuvta*] and for the additional amount [*tosefta*] to be paid out of the best part of my estate, both real estate and personal property that is mine under the heavens, whether I possess it now or whether I shall acquire in the future. All my property shall be mortgageable to defray this basic amount [*ketvuta*] and the additional amount

נוסח שטר כתובה

בְּאֶחָד (בַּשְּׁלִישִׁי) בְּשַׁבָּת, אֶחָד עָשָׂר יוֹם (יָמִים)
לַחֹדֶשׁ . . . .,, שְׁנַת חֲמֵשֶׁת אֲלָפִים וְשֵׁשׁ מֵאוֹת וְ . . . .
לִבְרִיאַת עוֹלָם לְמִנְיָן שֶׁאָנוּ מוֹנִין כָּאן ק"ק (עִיר) . . . .
בִּמְדִינַת אֲמֶרִיקָה הַצְּפוֹנִית, אֵיךְ הֶחָתָן ר' פ' בֶּן ר'
פ' (הַכֹּהֵן) אָמַר לָהּ לַהֲדָא בְּתוּלְתָּא פ' בַּת ר' פ',
הֱוִאי לִי לְאִנְתּוּ כְּדַת מֹשֶׁה וְיִשְׂרָאֵל, וַאֲנָא אֶפְלַח וְאוֹקִיר
וְאֵיזוּן וַאֲפַרְנֵס יָתִיכִי (לִיכִי) כְּהִלְכוֹת גּוּבְרִין יְהוּדָאִין
דְּפָלְחִין וּמוֹקְרִין וְזָנִין וּמְפַרְנְסִין לִנְשֵׁיהוֹן בְּקוּשְׁטָא.
וִיהֵיבְנָא לִיכִי מוֹהַר בְּתוּלַיְכִי כֶּסֶף זוּזֵי מָאתָן דְּחֲזֵי
לִיכִי מִדְּאוֹרַיְתָא, וּמְזוֹנַיְכִי וּכְסוּתַיְכִי וְסִפּוּקַיְכִי,
וּמֵיעַל לְוָתַיְכִי כְּאוֹרַח כָּל אַרְעָא. וּצְבִיאַת מָרַת פ'
בְּתוּלְתָּא דָא וַהֲוַת לֵיהּ לְאִנְתּוּ, וְדֵין נְדוּנְיָא דְּהַנְעֶלַת
לֵיהּ מִבֵּי אֲבוּהָ בֵּין בְּכֶסֶף בֵּין בְּדַהַב בֵּין בְּתַכְשִׁיטִין
בְּמָאנֵי דִלְבוּשָׁא, בְּשִׁימוּשֵׁי דִירָה וּבְשִׁימוּשֵׁי דְעַרְסָא,
הַכֹּל קִבֵּל עָלָיו ר' פ' חֲתַן דְּנָן בְּמֵאָה זְקוּקִים כֶּסֶף
צָרוּף. וּצְבִי ר' פ' חֲתַן דְּנָן וְהוֹסִיף לָהּ מִן דִּילֵיהּ עוֹד
מֵאָה זְקוּקִים כֶּסֶף צָרוּף אֲחֵרִים כְּנֶגְדָן, סַךְ הַכֹּל
מָאתַיִם זְקוּקִים כֶּסֶף צָרוּף.וְכָךְ אָמַר ר' פ' חֲתַן דְּנָן,
אַחֲרָיוּת שְׁטַר כְּתוּבְתָּא דָא, נְדוּנְיָא דֵין וְתוֹסֶפְתָּא דָא
קַבְּלִית עֲלַי וְעַל יָרְתַי בַּתְרַאי לְהִתְפָּרַע מִן כָּל שְׁפַר
אֲרַג נִכְסִין וְקִנְיָנִין דְּאִית לִי תְּחוֹת כָּל שְׁמַיָּא, דְּקְנָאִי
וּדְעָתִיד אֲנָא לְמִקְנֵא, נִכְסִין דְּאִית לְהוֹן אַחֲרָיוּת

[*tosefta*] even the mantle on my shoulders from now and for ever."

Thus the bridegroom, _____, took upon himself the aforesaid responsibility, with the restrictions applicable to all basic and additional marriage contracts made on behalf of Jewish wives according to the regulations of our sages and not drawn up without serious intent or merely as a blank form.

And this contract between the bridegroom, _____, and the bride, _____, comprising all that has been stated and explained above, was duly executed by means of this symbolic delivery [*kinyan*] of an object fit for that purpose, and everything is valid and binding.

Signed

_____ Witness   _____ Witness   _____ Groom

וּדְלֵית לְהוֹן אַחֲרָיוּת, כֻּלְּהוֹן יְהוֹן אַחֲרָאִין וְעַרְבָאִין
לִפְרוֹעַ מִנְּהוֹן שְׁטָר כְּתוּבְתָּא דָא, נְדוּנְיָא דֵין וְתוֹסֶפְתָּא
דָא מִנַּאי, וַאֲפִילוּ מִן גְּלִימָא דְעַל כַּתְפַּאי, בְּחַיַּי וּבָתַר
חַיַּי, מִן יוֹמָא דְנָן וּלְעָלַם. וְאַחֲרָיוּת שְׁטָר כְּתוּבְתָּא דָא,
נְדוּנְיָא דֵין וְתוֹסֶפְתָּא דָא, קַבֵּל עָלָיו ר׳ פ׳ חָתָן דְּנָן
כְּחוֹמֶר כָּל שְׁטָרֵי כְּתוּבוֹת וְתוֹסֶפְתוֹת דְּנָהֲגִין בִּבְנוֹת
יִשְׂרָאֵל, הָעֲשׂוּיִין כְּתִקּוּן חֲכָמֵינוּ זִכְרוֹנָם לִבְרָכָה, דְּלָא
כְאַסְמַכְתָּא וּדְלָא כְּטוֹפְסֵי דִשְׁטָרֵי. וְקָנִינָא מִן ר׳ פ׳
בֶּן פ׳ (הַכֹּהֵן) חָתָן דְּנָן לְמָרַת פ׳ בַּת ר׳ פ׳ בְּתוּלְתָּא
דָא עַל כָּל מַה דְּכָתוּב וּמְפוֹרָשׁ לְעֵיל בְּמָנָא דְכָשֵׁר
לְמִקְנָא בֵיהּ, וְהַכֹּל שָׁרִיר וְקַיָּם.

נְאוּם פ׳ בֶּן פ׳ עֵד.

וּנְאוּם פ׳ בֶּן פ׳ עֵד.

Alternative Ketubbah

On the _____ day of the week, the _____ day of _____, five thousand seven hundred and ____ years since the creation of the world as we reckon herein,

The bride _____, daughter of _____
Says to the groom: "With this ring, you are consecrated to me as my husband according to the law of Moses and the Jewish people. I shall treasure you, nourish you, support you, and respect you as Jewish women have devoted themselves to their husbands with integrity."

The groom _____, son of _____
Says to the bride: "With this ring, you are consecrated to me as my wife according to the law of Moses and the Jewish people. I shall treasure you, nourish you, support you, and respect you as Jewish men have devoted themselves to their wives with integrity."

We promise to be ever open to one another while cherishing each other's uniqueness to comfort and challenge each other. Through life's sorrow and joy to share our intuition and insight with one another and above all to do everything within our power to permit each of us to become the one we are yet to be.

We also pledge to establish a home open to the spiritual potential in all life. A home wherein the flow of the seasons and the passages of life are celebrated through the symbols of our Jewish heritage. A home filled with reverence for learning, loving, and generosity. A home wherein the ancient melody, candles, and wine sanctify the table, a home joined ever more closely to the community of Israel.

This marriage has been authorized by the civil authorities of _____ and is valid and binding.

Signed

_____ Witnesses   _____ Groom   _____ Bride   _____ Rabbi

ביום

בשבת

שנת חמשת

כאן   מונים   שאנו   העולם

לחדש

אלפים שבע מאת

לבריאת

ב

הכלה

בת   בן

החתן

את   הרי   לכלה   אומר   אתה   הרי   לחתן   אומרת

זו   בטבעת   לי   מקודשת   זו   בטבעת   לי   מקודש

ואני   וישראל   משה   כדת   וישראל   משה   כדת

אפלחך   לך   נאמן   אהיה   לך   נאמנה   אהיה   ואני

בכבוד   ואסעדך   אזונך   ואסעדך   אזונך   אפלחך

יהודיים   גברים   כמשפט   נשים   כמשפט   בכבוד

נשותיהם   את   האוהבים   את   האוהבות   יהודיות

בקושטא   בקושטא   בעליהן

אנחנו מבטיחים להיות כנים וגלויים זה עם זו לנצר את המיוחד
באישיותו של כל אחד מאתנו לסמוך איש את רעותו באתגרי
החיים בשעות צער ובשעות שמחה להיות שותפים בחכמה
ובתבונה שנחנו בהם ויותר מכל להשתדל בכל מאודנו לאפשר
לכל   אחד   מאתנו   להשיג   את   יעודו

אנחנו מקבלים עלינו להקים בית בו השכינה שורה בית
בו הזמנים והמועדים נהוגים על פי המורשה היהודית
בית מוקדש לתלמוד־תורה לצדקה ולגמילות חסדים בית
בו מהרהרים לניגונים עתיקים בו נרות ויין
לקידוש מעטרים את השולחן בית המהוה
חוליה בכלל   ישראל   ולעם   ישראל

נשואים אלה אושרו על ידי השלטונות האזרחיים
ב
והכל שריר וקיים

עד   עד

הכלה   החתן

הרב

63

Readings and Meditations

Brit (Covenant)

God's Love

At Sinai, God was the groom, Israel the bride, Torah the marriage contract and Moses the best man!
(Pirke de Rabbi Eliezer)

Helpmate

The Eternal God said, "It is not good for Man to be alone: I will make a fitting helper for him." So the Eternal God cast a deep sleep upon the Man and he slept; and God took one of his ribs and closed up the flesh at that spot. And the Eternal God fashioned into a woman the rib that God had taken from the Man and God brought her to the Man. Then the Man said: "This one at last is bone of my bones and flesh of my flesh., This one shall be called Woman for from Man was she taken." Hence a Man leaves his father and mother and clings to his wife, so that they become one flesh.
(Genesis 2:18, 21–24)

The *ketubbah* of Moses Aaron, son of Abraham from Cave and Flaminia, daughter of Abraham of Castro, Rome, 1780. This contract, with an undulating lower outline, is illustrated with floral shoots surmounted by a crown (BL MS Or. 12377E).

Rejoicing with the Bride and Groom

I greatly rejoice in the Eternal One,
My whole being exults in my God.
For God has clothed me in garments of triumph,
Wrapped me in a robe of victory
Like a bridegroom adorned with a turban,
Like a bride bedecked with her finery.

As a youth espouses a maiden
Your sons shall espouse you
And as a bridegroom rejoices over his bride,
So will your God rejoice over you.
   (Isaiah 61:10, 62:5)

Passion

I am a rose of Sharon,
A lily of the valleys.
Like a lily among the thorns,
So is my darling among the maidens.
Like an apple tree among trees of the forest,
So is my beloved among the youths.
I delight to sit in his shade,
And his fruit is sweet to my mouth.
My beloved spoke to me thus,
Arise my love,
My fair one, come away,
For now the winter is past,
The rains are over and gone;
The blossoms have appeared in the land,
The time of pruning has come,

The song of the turtledove
Is heard in our land;
The green figs form on the fig tree,
The vines in blossom give off fragrance
Arise, my love,
My fair one, come away

Let me be a seal upon your heart
Like the seal upon your hand:
For love is as fierce as death;
Passion is mighty as Sheol:
It's darts are darts of fire,
A blazing flame.
Vast floods cannot quench love,
Not rivers drown it.

    (Song of Songs, 2:1–3, 10–13, 8: 6–7)

May it Be

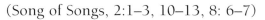

May joys be many in Israel
    May consolations be many in Israel
    May salvation be many in Israel
May good tidings be many in Israel
May love multiply in Israel
May blessings multiply in Israel
May rejoicing multiply in Israel
May joys multiply in Israel
May splendor multiply in Israel
May bridegrooms be many in Israel
May brides be many in Israel
As of this day and in Jerusalem, may they rejoice and be glad.
May Elijah the prophet come to us soon.

    (From the Karaite marriage ritual, eighth century)

Joy and Sorrow Commingled

I shatter the glass, bride of my heart
I shatter the glass for our land that lies broken
For our beautiful city whose name is a part
Of the vows we have just spoken

I shatter the glass, bride of my life
For our joys must be dyed in the tears of a sorrow
In the smiles of a hope, O my child, O my wife
Wistful still for the morrow

I shatter your heart, bride of my soul
I break it and pour it, unmeasured libation
Till the cup of our people be brimming and whole
With the wine of salvation

    (Jessie Sampter, twentieth century, USA and Israel)

Ahava (Love)

Love is a Promise

To love someone is not just a strong feeling; it is a decision, it is a judgment, it is a promise. If love were only a feeling, there would be no basis for the promise to love each other forever. A feeling comes and goes. How can I judge that it will last forever when my act does not involve judgment and decision?

    Love is only possible if two persons communicate with each other from the center of their existence. Only in this central experience is human reality, only here is aliveness, only here is the basis of love. Love experienced thus is a constant challenge, it is not a resting place, but a moving, growing, working together; even though there is harmony or conflict, joy or sadness, it is secondary to the fundamental fact that two people experience themselves from the essence of their existence that they are one with each other by being one with themselves. There is only one proof for the presence of love; the depth of the relationship and the aliveness and strength of each person concerned; this is the fruit by which love is recognized.

(Erich Fromm, *The Art of Loving*)

Independent Love

Any love which is contingent on a thing, when the thing is nullified the love disintegrates; but a love which is independent of anything will never disintegrate. What is the prototype of love, which is contingent on a thing? This is the love of Amnon and Tamar. And what is the prototype of a love, which is independent of anything? This is the love of David and Jonathan.

(Pirke Avot 5:19)

Love's Joy

To love is to see the world through the eye of the other. It is to be patient with the temperament of the other. To love is to suffer the pain of the other and open one's self to the possibility of being hurt by the other. For who can hurt me more than someone I love? Yet who can give me joy more than someone I love?

(Anonymous)

Kiddushin (Holiness)

Mystic Union

From every human being there rises a light that reaches straight to heaven. And when two souls that are destined to be together find each other, their streams of light flow together, and a single brighter light goes forth from their united being. (Baal Shem Tov)

A Bride's Plea

Almighty God! Soon I shall come to You, by the side of him whom you have sent to me to be my consort of life. The solemn moment is fast approaching that shall forever unite me with the beloved of my heart. Oh, how my heart throbs, how it pulsates between fear and hope! For I know the importance and solemnity of this moment. I know that henceforth my life will assume another form, that I take upon myself new sacred duties that are often difficult to fulfill. Therefore I pray to You from the depth of my heart: Assist me! Be my guide, my shield, and protector in all my paths. Grant that I may remain united with my companion of life in unceasing fidelity and undisturbed harmony!

Direct all our destinies into blessings and guard us against all trials and tribulations. Make the days of our united life to be days of happiness, tranquillity, and contentment. Grant that our union may be a rich source of virtue, of pious joy, and mutual bliss. Be merciful to us even in later days that we may with joyful and happy hearts look back upon this solemn day and remember You with gratitude.

Amen.

(*Studen der Andacht*, compiled by Fanny Neuda, 1859)

Completion and Blessing

Marriage is not a one-sided affair. The man has obligations no less than the woman. First he must have as high a regard for his wife as for his own self and honor her accordingly. She brings him completion and blessing, and it is his duty to realize it. He must be particularly careful to provide the needs of the home; for lack of provision is often the beginning of strife. Above all let him treat his wife with love and sympathy, seeing she is a part of him and depends on him as he depends upon God.

(Israel ibn Al-Nakawa, fourteenth century)

The Ideal Husband

Happy are those who fear the Eternal, who walk in God's ways.
When you eat the produce of your hands, happy shall you be and it will go well with you

Your wife shall be like a fruitful vine within your house
Your children like shoots of the olive tree around your table
Surely this is how a man is blessed, who fears the Eternal One
May the Eternal bless you from Zion, may you see the good of
Jerusalem all the days of your life
and see your children's children. Peace upon Israel
    (Psalm 128)

The Ideal Wife

A woman of worth is hard to find for she is more precious
than rubies
Her husband trusts her in his heart without losing from it
All the days of her life she brings him good not harm
Her children rise to revere her
And her husband sings her praises
Many women have done great deeds, but you surpass them all
Charm is a delusion and beauty fades
The woman who reveres God is to be praised
Esteem her for the work of her hands
And her own good deeds will praise her in public
    (Proverbs 31:10–12, 29–31)

Mystical Reunion

Each soul and spirit prior to its entering into this world
consists of a male and female united into one being. When
it descends on this earth, the two parts separate and

animate into two different bodies. At the time of marriage, the Holy One who knows all souls and spirits unites them again as they were before and again constitute one body and one soul.

(Zohar 1:91b)

Index of Readings

Al-Nakawa, Israel ibn *Completion and Blessing* 71

Anonymous *Love's Joy* 69

Avot, Pirke 5:19 *Independent Love* 69

Baal Shem Tov *Mystic Union* 70

Eliezer, Pirke de Rabbi, *God's Love* 65

Fromm, Erich, *Love is a Promise* 68

Genesis 2:18,21–24, *Helpmate* 65

Isaiah 61:10, 62:5, *Rejoicing with Bride and Groom* 66

Karaite marriage ritual, *May It Be* 67

Proverbs 31:10–12, 29–31 *The Ideal Wife* 72

Psalm 128 *The Ideal Husband* 71

Sampter, Jessie, *Joy and Sorrow Comingled* 68

Song of Songs 2:1–3, 10–13, 8:6–7 *Passion* 66

Studen der Andacht, *A Bride's Plea* 70

Zohar 1:91b *Mystical Reunion* 72

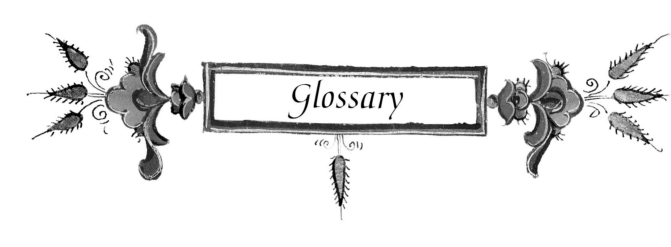

Glossary

Agunah—chained woman; a woman whose marriage has not been terminated by Jewish law

Ahava—love

Arayot—proscribed marriages

Aufruf—special honor of reading the Torah bestowed upon the couple in synagogue prior to their wedding day

Badchan—jester and master of ceremonies at the wedding festivities

Bedeken—the veiling of the bride prior to the wedding ceremony

Bi'ah—marriage by cohabitation; one of the three talmudic ways to marry

Brit—Covenant

Chatan—bridegroom

Chuppah—the wedding canopy

Erusin—betrothal

Get—a bill of divorce

Halitzah—ceremony of release from levirate marriage

Hiddur mitzvah—enhancement or adornment of the ritual commandments

Kallah—bride

Kesef—marriage by exchange of token of value; one of the three talmudic ways to marry

Ketubbah—the marriage contract

Kiddushin—holiness; the part of the Talmud dealing with marriage laws; also used to describe the act of marriage as part of the wedding nuptials

Kinyan—the act of agreeing to the marriage contract

Kittel—a white robe worn by groom

Mazal Tov—good luck, congratulations

Messader kiddushin—officiant at the wedding ceremony

Mikveh—ritual bath for immersion

Mitzvah—commandment; religious obligation

Mohar—purchase price for a bride in biblical times

Niddah—rabbinic laws of family purity

Nissuin—wedding nuptials

Sefer kritut—another name for the divorce document of *Get*

Sheva brachot—seven special blessings recited under the chuppah as well as at the wedding feast

Shidduchin—engagement; can also be used for arranged marriages

Shoshvin—groomsmen and attendants

Sh'tar—marriage by contract; one of the three talmudic ways to marry

Simchah—rejoicing; refers to the wedding festivities

Tallith—prayer shawl

Tenaim—conditions, formal engagement contracts

Yihud—seclusion; a moment of privacy for the newly married couple immediately following the wedding ceremony

After the Ceremony

The festive wedding meal (*simchah*) is enjoyed as a *seudah mitzvah*—an opportunity to rejoice. It dates back to the time of Jacob's marriage to Leah when Laban sponsored such a feast (Genesis 29:22). During the Middle Ages, singing and dancing were incorporated into the wedding festivities and a *badchan* or jester was often invited to host the entertainment. As the celebrations increased in size and expense, medieval rabbis of Northern Europe expressed concern at the lavish parties and display of wealth. They issued rabbinic ordinances forbidding extravagant parties, but did not always succeed at tempering the spirit of joy and celebration.

The wedding Grace after Meals incorporates some special elements including a short poem asking for the banishment of sorrow at such a happy time:

> *Banish sorrow and all anguish*
> *Then even the mute will rejoice in song*
> *Lead us in the paths of righteousness*
> *Accept the blessing of the Children of Israel*

The *sheva brachot* are recited, often by honored guests. The blessing for wine is recited last and the leader mixes two glasses of wine from which the bride and groom drink. For seven days, the *sheva brachot* are recited at special bridal parties in friends' homes. Thus a week of rejoicing is concluded and life for the new married couple begins in earnest!

Acknowledgments

With thanks to Michael Brunström and Anne Fraser for their encouragement and pursuit of this book. I am indebted to Rabbi John Rayner for sharing his unpublished manuscript on Jewish marriage with me and for its erudition and accuracy, which I can only hope to emulate.

In fond remembrance of May 26th 1991/13 Sivan 5751 and all who were there to celebrate with Marcia and me.

Michael J. Shire

Details of the manuscripts by Ilana Tahan, curator, Hebrew Section, British Library

Published in 2002 by
Stewart, Tabori & Chang
A Company of La Martinière Groupe
115 West 18th Street
New York, NY 10011

Canadian Distribution:
Canadian Manda Group
One Atlantic Avenue, Suite 105
Toronto, Ontario M6K 3E7
Canada

Library of Congress Catalog Number: 2002109891

ISBN: 1-58479-259-0

The text of this book was composed in Berkeley and Medici Script

Printed in Singapore

10 9 8 7 6 5 4 3 2 1
First Printing